PLAYAOLOGY

BY

PRETTY TONY

Published by
WORLD MOVEMENT PUBLISHING

www.worldmovement.com

All rights reserved

Copyright © **2011 by Pretty Tony**

**No part of this book may be reproduced
or transmitted in any form**

**Or any means, electronic, or mechanical, including
photocopying, Recording, or by any information storage
and retrieval system,**

Without permission in writing from the author.

For information contact

lamont@worldmovement.com

prettytonylv@gmail.com

ISBN # 978-09828768-2-4

www.playasuniversitysygu.com

Printed in the U.S.A

PLAYAOLOGY

PLAYA STEP YOUR GAME UP . VOL II

DEFINITION OF THE LIFE STYLE

BY PRETTY TONY

THIS IS THE DEFINITION OF THE PLAYA LIFESTYLE, DUE TO MOVIES, MUSIC VIDEOS, EVERYONE IS NOW IN THE BUSINESS OF GLORIFYING THE GENTLEMAN OF LEISURE LIFESTYLE, BUT NOBODY IS DEFINING IT, PUTTING THE REAL RULES OF BEING A PLAYA OUT THERE, TELLING THE PROS AND THE CONS OF THE LIFESTYLE.

THAT IS LIKE GIVING A BLIND MAN A BOOK AND TELLING HIM TO READ IT, TO PARTAKE OF THIS LIFE YOU MUST LIVE IT, BREATHE IT, YOU MUST LEARN TO ENGAGE AND LURE OUR OBJECTIVES THAT OF COURSE BEING WOMEN.

BUT BEFORE YOU SET OUT ON THIS QUEST, STEP INTO THE CLASSROOM, PLAYA STEP YOUR GAME UP WAS THE INTRODUCTORY COURSE THIS IS THE DEGREE PROGRAM.

PLAYAOLOGY 101…

NEVER STEP ONTO THE PLAYING FIELD UNTIL YOU KNOW THE GAME BEING PLAYED AND THE RULES…

ACKNOWLEDGEMENTS

MY POPS ADDIE THE FIRST PLAYA I EVER KNEW, 'THE BRONX MASSIVE' MY ORIGINAL CREW, ALCA-POOLE, FACE, WAFFLE, BOGART, BOBO, BURGER, GANJA BABY, GARFEILD, DOOGS, FLEMMINGS, OWLY, ANGLIN, ONE LOVE.

MY MIAMI FAMILIA, BRUCE, (KEEP YA HEAD UP)

CRACK DA COMEDIAN, STILL GOT LUV FOR YA, RANDY & THE CODNER FAMILY BIG UPS TO SKINNY, CURLY DREAD, JAKE, AND ALL THE NEICES AND NEPHEWS, MY L.A FAMILY LUCKY LUCK, BABY RAY, M&M, SCOOTER, TERRY, BIGG MACC, DELAGADO, XAVIER, TO THE WORLD MOVEMENT PUBLISHING FAMILY THAT MADE THE DREAM REAL, LAMONT PATTERSON MUCH LOVE….

HONORARY MENTIONS

DAMION, MY LITTLE BROTHER, MY CUZZO MARK, WIMPY, DONALD, SAMMY, QUENTIN, OMAR, JUNIOR, GEORGE VICKERS, SAMUEL BARRETT, HAROLD ADAMS, ALRICK, SOPHIA…R.I.P TO EACH ONE OF YOU.

TO MY SUGA, SUGAS, ALL OVER THE WORLD, WHAT WOULD LIFE BE WITHOUT YOU, POP YOUR THONG ONE TIME FOR ME…"OH SO SEXY"

CONTENT

SINCE I'M A BOSS PLAYA THIS BOOK IS WRITTEN THE WAY I WANT IT TO BE, NO CHAPTERS JUST STRAIGHT GAME, UNCUT, HIGH GRADE LIKE SOME PURE FISH SCALES, SO I'M DROPPIN THIS GAME BY THE GRAMS, OUNCES, AND KILOS, SOAK IT UP SQUARES AND PLAYAS PROFESSOR PUSSINGTON IS NOW IN THE BUILDING............................

OPENING LECTURE

HOW MANY OF YOU BROTHERS OUT THERE SPEND ALL YOUR TIME FLOSSIN, BUT DON'T OWN A THING, CARS WITH RIMS, BUMPING SOUND SYSTEMS, EXPENSIVE ACCESSORIES ON A CHEAP CAR, AND ALWAYS ASKING FOR GAS MONEY.

WHAT IS WRONG WITH YOU? YOU HAVE NO GOALS, NO GAME PLAN, YOUR PRIORITIES ARE SCREWED UP, YOU SPEND ALL YOUR TIME CHASING SKIRT, POPPPIN BOTTLES, AND TRYING TO LIVE UP TO MUSIC VIDEOS AND URBAN MYTHS. EVERY SKIRT YOU SEE YOU'RE ALL OVER IT. FOR WHAT?? A FEW MOMENTS OF SEXUAL PLEASURE AND MOMENTARY SATISFACTION, THEN YOU'RE RIGHT BACK TO BEING BROKE. FLOSSIN IS FOR KIDS GET OUT OF LOLLIPOP LAND, LITTLE BOY.

TO BE REAL IN THIS GAME ,YOU MUST HAVE 'HUSTLERS AMBITION, THE MINDSET THAT I MUST TRIPLE MY WORTH. THE MOTTO IS "MAKING MONEY MATERIALIZE MAKES LIFE EASIER!"

TRUE STORY, ONE OF MY HOMEYS MADE SOME MOVES AND HIT A COUPLE CORNERS TO INCREASE THE GWAP (CASH) FLOW. THE MOVES WERE FRUITFUL AND A COUPLE GRAND WAS NOW IN THE MIX. FIRST MOVE WAS OLD SCHOOL CADILLAC BROUGHHAM, TWO DOOR, TRICKED OUT WITH BLACK ON BLACK CANDY PAINT JOB, CUSTOM UPHOLSTERY, ALPINE SOUNDS, SITTTIN ON DANA DANES, DAYTONS FOR YOU SQUARES.

HE WAS NOW OFFICIALLY GHETTO FABULOUS, BUT EVERYTIME HE CUT THE CAR OFF HE HAD TO POP THE HOOD GET AN OLD GALLON WATER BOTTLE THAT HE KEPT GAS IN AND POUR A LITTLE GAS IN THE CARBURETOR, THAT IS DAMN SURE PUTTING THE CART BEFORE THE

HORSE, WHAT WAS THIS FOOL THINKING , HE COULD HAVE BEEN JACKED ANYWHERE, ANYTIME, ALL BECAUSE HE DIDN'T HAVE THE RIGHT MINDSET, A LOT OF SQUARES AND WANNABES ARE DISRESPECTING THE GAME, YOU HAVE TO BE IN IT TO WIN IT, AND IF YOU'RE NOT HANDLING YOUR BUSINEES THEN THE GAME WILL HAVE YOU REPLACED, BECAUSE TRUTH BE TOLD THE GAME NEVER STOPS FOR ANYONE.

SO HERE IS A LIST OF THINGS THAT SHOW YOU'RE NOT A PLAYA:

IF YOU LIVE IN YOUR BABYMOMMA'S SECTION 8 HOUSING UNIT.

STAYING IN YOUR PARENTS' HOME AND NOT PAYING YOUR WAY .

BORROWING YOUR FRIEND'S CAR TO FLOSS WHEN YOU REALLY OWN A BUS PASS.

CUBIC ZIRCONIA AND COSTUME JEWELRY ARE YOUR DAILY ACCESSORIES.

BORROWING YOUR HOMEYS CLOTHES TO WEAR OUT.

YOU'RE OVER 18 AND HAVE NO INCOME AND NOTHING STASHED.

NEVER TRAVELLED ANYWHERE AND DON'T PLAN TO .

CAN'T SEQUENCE WORDS TO EXPRESS A THOUGHT, LET ALONE HOLD A CONVERSATION.

DRIVING A BREEZY'S CAR AND DON'T OWN ONE OF YOUR OWN.

PAYING WOMEN'S RENT AND GETTING VERY LITTLE IN RETURN (YOU'RE A TRICK)

NOT A POT TO PISS IN OR WINDOW TO THROW IT OUT.

SLEEPING ON WOMEN'S COUCHES OR IN THEIR BED BUT HAVE NO PLACE OF YOUR OWN.

EVERYTIME YOUR FRIENDS OR FAMILY SEE YOU IT'S A BEGGING SPREE . YOU MY FRIEND ARE NOT A PLAYA!

WHAT IS A PLAYA ?

WHAT SEPARATES A PLAYA FROM THOSE AROUND HIM?

DOES SLEEPING WITH A BUNCH OF WOMEN MAKE YOU A PLAYA?

NO! YOU'RE A SCRUB IN PLAYAS CLOTHING.

A PLAYA HAS HIS OWN, AND IS ALWAYS MAKIN MOVES TO INCREASE THE GWAP FLOW,

HE'S DEFINED BY THE FACT THAT HE"S ALWAYS IS IN THE FLOW OF EVERYTHING,

HE'S THE CAT THAT EVERYONE WANTS TO BE, HE NAVIGATES THRU HIS ENVIRONMENT WITH EASE, LATEST TRENDS, AND OF COURSE LADY FRIENDS, A WOMAN COMES INTO HIS LIFE FOR ADDITION NOT SUBTRACTION A PLAYA COMES INTO HER LIFE TO GIVE HER FREEDOM, YES, FREEDOM.

BUT OTHER SQUARES TRIED TO PUT SHACKLES ON HER, WE APPRECIATE HER, NEVER PARTAKING IN DEPRECIATION OF HER STATUS, WE DO NOT PARTICIPATE IN THE DRAMA OF EVERYDAY LIFE, EVERYBODY AROUND US KNOWS THEIR ROLE AND PLAYS THEIR ROLE, DRAMA IS KEPT TO A MINIMUM. HATING IS NEVER FASHIONABLE.

THE GEAULXDEN RULES

THOU SHALT NOT BE BROKE.
THOU SHALT NOT HATE ON ANOTHER PLAYA.
THOU SHALT NOT HANDCUFF A HONEY TO YOUR HIPS.
JEALOUSY IS A CHILDISH TRAIT.
A PLAYA ALWAYS STRIVES TO ACQUIRE THE FINER THINGS IN LIFE.
FEMININE GENEROSITY IS A MUST FOR OUR FEMALE COMPANIONS.
THAT WHICH WE CHOOSE TO GIVE IS NEVER NEEDED BACK.
GOSSIPING IS LEFT TO THOSE WITH TOO MUCH TIME ON THEIR HANDS, WE'RE TOO BUSY SHINING.
IF IT AIN'T ABOUT SOMETHING IT AIN'T FOR US.
STRIPES ARE EARNED NEVER GIVEN.
IF SHE'S NOT LISTENING TO WHAT I SAY SHE'S NOT IN THE PROGRAM.

YOU MUST LET WOMEN KNOW THAT NOTHING ADDED NOTHING LEAVES NOTHING.

WHEN DEALING WITH WOMEN YOU MUST UNDERSTAND THAT SHE IS USED TO DEALING WITH JEALOUS, INSECURE MEN.

THEY TRIED TO TEAR HER DOWN, HOLD HER BACK, FRUSTRATE HER, DISTRACT HER FROM HER SUCCESS, HE CALLED HER IDEAS STUPID TO HUMILIATE HER BECAUSE OF HIS INSECURITIES, BUT AS A PLAYA YOUR JOB IS TO MOTIVATE HER, ENCOURAGE HER, TO LET HER KNOW THE SKY IS THE LIMIT, AND IF SHE WANTS TO REACH FOR THE STARS TELL HER TO GO FOR IT, UPLIFT HER MENTALITY, TELL HER THAT HER DREAMS ARE GOING TO BECOME REALITY, HER SUCCESS IS THEN YOUR

SUCCESS BECAUSE A PLAYAS TIME IS NEVER FREE, THE INSPIRATION YOU PROVIDE IS IMPORTANT TO HER WELL BEING, TO BENEFIT FROM "WOMEN INC." YOU MUST INVEST IT.

IT IS THE WORLD'S LARGEST CORPORATION WITH UNLIMITED RESOURCES, WOMEN ARE ON THE INSIDE OF ANYTHING AND EVERYTHING YOU WANT OR NEED, PILLOW TALK AND BEDROOM ESCAPADES ARE WHERE WE MEN ARE AT OUR WEAKEST, EMPIRES HAVE BEEN BROUGHT DOWN TO THEIR KNEES BY THE POWER OF THE VAGINA.

AS A PLAYA YOU BETTER KNOW AND UNDERSTAND THE POWER YOU'RE DEALING WITH. MEN HAVE SOLD THEIR VERY SOULS FOR ESSENCE OF LIFE THAT LIES BETWEEN A WOMAN'S LEGS AND ONCE YOU UNDERSTAND THE POWER, YOU KNOW HOW TO HARNESS ITS BENEFITS .

A SQUARE WILL GO OUT AND WORK HARD EVERYDAY OF THE YEAR TO GAIN SUCCESS, AND WHEN THE FRUITS OF HIS LABOR PAY OFF HIS FIRST INSTINCT IS TO FIND A WOMAN TO SHARE IT WITH. WHEN SHE GETS HOLD OF HIM AND PERFUMES HER BODY TO HIS LIKING, SHE WILL MESMERIZE HIM, MANIPULATE HIM, AND 'PUDAZZLE' HIM. SHE WILL STRUT AROUND IN ATTIRE TO DRIVE HIM CRAZY.

SHE WILL LAY MOIST JUICY KISSES ON HIS BODY. SHE WILL TOUCH HIM TO HIS LIKING GENTLY OR ROUGH PRESS HER SOFT BREASTS AGAINST HIM NOW HE'S LIKE A VOLCANO ABOUT TO ERUPT AND IN THAT VERY MOMENT SHE HAS HIM GONE, BEFORE YOU KNOW IT SHE HAS THE GATE CODE, ALARM CODE, KEY TO THE CRIB AND CAR, MOST IMPORTANTLY THE PIN NUMBER TO THE ATM CARD.

WOMEN ARE POWERFUL, GET THIS THRU YOUR HEAD, VAGINA IS ADDICTIVE IT CAN TAKE YOU ON A WILD RIDE OUT OF THIS WORLD.

EVERY MAN REMEMBERS THAT ONE GIRL WHO DID THE FREAKIEST THINGS TO YOU SHE WOULD MAKE YOUR KNEES SHAKE, SHE STAYS IN THE BACK OF YOUR MIND.

SHE ROCKED YOU TILL YOU WERE LIMP.

'YOU REMEMBER HER DON'T YOU?'

AND IF YOU'VE NEVER HAD ONE OF THESE EXPERIENCES I'M SORRY FOR YOU!

SOME FOOLS GET SO WIDE OPEN THEY PROPOSE MARRIAGE TO A GIRL LIKE THAT YOU CAN'T TAME A FORCE OF NATURE LIKE THAT.

SHE WILL HAVE YOU PARKED DOWN THE BLOCK WITH BINOCULARS, STALKING HER, CHECKING HER PHONE, SMELLING HER PANTIES, SHE WILL RAVAGE YOUR MIND, RAVAGE YOUR BODY, RAVAGE YOUR VERY SOUL, TOYING WITH YOUR EMOTIONS.

SEARCHING FOR HER IN THE DAY LIGHT WITH A FLASHLIGHT

'RESPECT THE POWER OF A WOMAN'S SEXUALITY.'

WHEN YOU GET IN TAKE IT ALL IN STRIDE LET THE GAME COME TO YOU, KNOW WHEN YOU'RE GETTING IN TOO DEEP. NOW LET ME TAKE A QUICK SIDEBAR TO CLEAR UP SOME MISCONCEPTIONS, A PIMP AND A PLAYA ARE TWO DIFFERENT BREEDS THERE ARE SIMILARITIES BUT MAJOR DIFFERENCES MAINLY A PIMPS' MAIN SOURCE OF

INCOME IS THE WOMEN IN HIS CARE, A PLAYAS' GAME IS MORE SPREADOUT HE HAS DIFFERENT HUSTLES INCLUDING THE GENEROSITY OF HIS LADY FRIENDS, WE SHARE THE SAME P.I.M.P MINDSET PERSISTENTLY IN MONETARY PURSUITS, AND AN UNDERSTANDING THAT EACH DAY IS COMMITED TO THESE PURSUITS, MY NICKNAME IS 'JOHNNY PAPERCHASE' AKA 'CHARLIE HUSTLE' SO ANYONE GETTING THEIR GRIND ON POP YA COLLAR ONE TIME WITH A CERTIFIED WINNER .

PLAYAISM

A FOOL AND HIS MONEY ARE SOON PARTED.

LIVE WITHIN YOUR MEANS.

A PLAYA IS A THINKER BECAUSE THE GAME CHANGES RAPIDLY SO YOU GOT TO BE QUICK, I'M SPITTING THIS GAME AT YOU SO KEEP UP, TO STAY ON TOP OF THE GAME, YOU HAVE TO SEE THE BIG PICTURE STAY ACTIVE MENTALLY, REAL MEN DO THE THINGS THEY SAY, LITTLE BOYS SAY THE THINGS THEY'RE GOING TO DO.

'REAL TALK'

THE BIG THING NOW IS YOUR BLING STATUS UNDERSTANDING THE THREE 'Cs' OF THE BLING GAME WILL PREVENT YOU INVESTING IN LOW QUALITY GEMS CLARITY, CUT, COLOR, ARE VERY IMPORTANT IN YOUR INVESTING, THIS DETERMINES THE VALUE OF YOUR 'ICE' VVS, Si 1, Si 2, J, H, WHAT COLOR, IS YOUR DIAMOND NATURAL OR LAB CREATED. WILL IT TRULY HOLD UP

TO THE APPRAISAL YOU GOT ? YOU CAN'T LISTEN TO SOMEBODY OF LESS INTELLIGENCE THAN YOURSELF ABOUT THE NATURE OF THE HUSTLE.

NOW TO THE LOVE OF MY LIFE 'WOMEN'

THERE IS SO MUCH TO KNOW ABOUT THEM AND SOME OF MY BROTHERS NEVER TOOK THE TIME TO DISCOVER THE INNERWORKING OF A WOMANS' MIND.

FELLAS, IF YOU DON'T TREASURE HER THEN ANOTHER CAT CALLED 'JOE GRIND' WILL, HE WANTS YOUR WOMAN, TO TOUCH HER, FEEL HER, NOW SOME OF YOU BUST A NUT AND ROLLOVER BROTHERS NEED TO STEP YOUR GAME UP, WHEN IS THE LAST TIME YOU GAVE YOUR WOMAN A FULL BODY MASSAGE, KISSED HER HAND SOFTLY, MASSAGED HER SCALP, WAITED FOR HER TO GET OUT THE SHOWER AND MOISTURISED HER BODY,?

A PLAYA KNOWS HIS WOMANS' BODY.

HE KNOWS HOW TO MAKE HER FEEL WANTED, REMEMBER THE WORD 'FOREPLAY' WARM HER UP, GET HER ENGINE GOING, THEN UNLEASH THE BEAST.

FIND OUT WHAT TYPE OF WOMAN SHE IS:
IS SHE ROUGH?
IS SHE GENTLE?
IS SHE A RIDER?
DOES SHE LIKE TO BE RIDDEN?
SOME WOMEN LIKE IT ANIMALISTIC,
SOME LIKE ROMANCE,
WHAT DOES YOUR GIRL LIKE?

A WOMAN ALWAYS LIKES TO FEEL THAT SHE HAS SOMETHING HER GIRLFRIENDS DON'T, TRUST ME, SHE

MAY FRONT LIKE THIS IS NOT TRUE, BUT IN THE BACK OF HER MIND, SHE'S LIKE NAH, NAH, NANANA.

LET'S KEEP IT MOVING RIGHT ALONG, I'M KIND OF IN THE MOOD FOR A SMALL COGNAC BREAK, BUT THE CLASS MUST GO ON.

THIS IS FOR YOU BROTHAS WHO FEEL THE NEED/URGE TO HIT WOMEN.

ARE YOU BIPOLAR ?

DO YOU HAVE SOME DEFICIENCY YOU'RE TRYING TO COMPENSATE FOR? YOUR INSECURITIES ARE PROBABLY GETTING THE BETTER OF YOU, HUH !

YOU NEED A SERIOUS REALITY CHECK. KEEPING A WOMAN IN FEAR IS NEVER A GOOD LOOK. AT SOME POINT A SMOOTH TALKING BROTHA WILL COME ALONG AND GIVE HER THE ATTENTION AND AFFECTION SHE'S CRAVING, AND YOU BEST BELIEVE SHE WILL BE GONE.

A WOMAN IS VALUABLE ASSET. TO ABUSE HER IS TO DAMAGE YOUR ACE IN THE HOLE THAT WOULD PROBABLY GO TO THE ENDS OF THE EARTH FOR YOU.

HOW MANY OF YOUR HOMIES WOULD DO THAT?

IF SHE DOES NOT MAKE YOU HAPPY ANYMORE LEAVE HER, DON'T HIT HER!

IF SHE POPS OFF AT THE LIP TOO MUCH, FIND A MORE COOPERATIVE WOMAN AND LEAVE HER. IF SHE'S GAINED TOO MUCH WEIGHT, LEAVE HER BUT DON'T BEAT HER!

IF SHE DOESN'T ACT THE WAY YOU WANT HER TO, STEP OFF AND LEAVE HER, BUT DO NOT ABUSE HER, DO NOT

HIT HER! I HAVE NEVER HIT A WOMAN IN MY LIFE! IF SHE'S NOT WHAT I NEED I KEEP IT MOVING! IF SHE'S NOT WILLING TO PLAY THE CARDS I'M LAYING OUT SHE HAS TO BE ON HER WAY.

BUT SOME OF YOU WANNABE PLAYAS DON'T GET THE GAME BECAUSE YOU JUST STARTED CLAIMING THE PLAYAS CARD.

THERE IS NO SUCH THING AS A 'POSSESSIVE' PLAYA

ARE YOU STUPID?

JEALOUSY, CONTROLLING, ABUSIVE, THESE WORDS ARE IN NO WAY ASSOCIATED WITH THE WORD PLAYA.

GET IT THROUGH YOUR HEAD 'YOU DO NOT OWN A WOMAN.' SHE IS WITH BECAUSE SHE 'CHOSE'.

SHE'S DOWN FOR YOU BECAUSE SHE WANTS TO ROLL WITH YOU. IF YOU WANT AN EXCLUSIVE RELATIONSHIP BECOME A ONE WOMAN MAN.

IF YOU'RE A PLAYA SET YOUR PROGRAM TELL HER GET WITH THE PROGRAM.

NOW YOU 'DOORMAT DANNY' CATS OUT THERE, THAT HAVE WOMEN TREATING YOU LIKE PUPPIES...SIT, JUMP, ROLL OVER, KISS MY FEET, DO THIS, DO THAT...DON'T TALK TO YOUR FRIENDS IF YOU LOVE ME, CHOOSE ME OVER EVERYTHING, IF YOU LOVE ME YOU WOULD SELL YOUR SOUL TO MAKE ME HAPPY...

DO YOU HAVE A BRAIN IMBALANCE?

DID YOUR MOMMA DOMINATE YOU?

DID YOUR BIG SISTER KICK YOUR ASS ?

NO...YOU'RE A GLUTTON FOR PUNISHMENT !

CHECK THIS OUT DANNY BOY.

WHATEVER IT IS THAT MAKES YOU TICK, IT'S TIME TO GRAB YOUR BALLS, AND SAY 'HONEY I'M TAKING MY BALLS BACK!'

LEARN THESE WORDS I'M A MAN NOT A DOORMAT!

ALLOW NO WOMAN TO WIPE HER FEET ON YOU, YOU'RE A GROWN ASS MAN ACT LIKE IT!

OKAY YOU WANTED A DIMEPEICE AND AND YOU GOT ONE BUT REALITY HAS SET IN AND YOU REALIZE THAT YOU'RE IN THE DEEP END AND CAN'T SWIM.

DON'T PANIC, GET YOUR GAME FACE ON, KISSING ASS DOES NOT GET YOU RESPECT.

THINK ABOUT IT.

A "YES" MAN IS JUST A PUPPET, BETTER YET A PUPPY.

'WHO'S A GOOD BOY?' 'DANNY WANT A TREAT ?'

DAMN I'M ON A ROLL NOW. NOW DON'T GET ME WRONG 'DANNY' IF LIKE LICKIN YOUR WOMANS' BOOTS AND HAVING HEELS DUG IN YOUR FLESH BRINGS YOU JOY, DO YOUR THING DAWG, BUT IF DEEP IN YOUR SOUL, YOU THINK I NEED TO SPEAK UP FOR MYSELF BUT I'M AFRAID SHE WILL LEAVE ME.

'DANNY', YOUR TIME HAS COME. MAKE THAT MOVE, SCREAM OUT "THIS IS WHO I AM"! "THIS IS HOW I ROLL!"

YOU'RE A MAN DAMN IT!

LET ME BLESS YOU WITH SOME MORE PLAYAISM.
YOU CATS THAT ARE ON THE 'DOWN LOW .'

COME THE HELL OUT THE CLOSET.

BE THE HELL WHO YOU ARE !

STOP PERPETRATING AND TOYING WITH YOUR WOMAN.

THIS IS THE 21ST CENTURY AND IF YOU'RE NOT BEING TRUE TO YOU THEN YOU'RE LIVING A LIE FOR SOMEONE ELSE AND THE WALLS WILL COME CRASHING DOWN BECAUSE THE TRUTH IS THAT YOU'RE BEING SELFISH.

SHE SIGNED UP TO BE WITH YOU, NOT TO BE WITH YOU AND YOUR MAN, IF THIS IS HOW YOU TRULY SEE YOURSELF TO BE, HANDLE THAT.

ENOUGH ABOUT YOU

'OH SNAP !' I CAN'T FORGET ABOUT THE CATS THAT BEEN HUSTLING FOR YEARS AND STILL BROKE, BUYING $50 DOUBLE UPS, FOR THE LAST TEN YEARS AND CAUGHT A COUPLE CASES...

YOU MIGHT NEED A CAREER CHANGE, GET A JOB WITH SOME BENEFITS, YOU'RE NOT GETTING ANY YOUNGER, SOMEBODY FORGET TO TELL YOU HUSTLING IS A COME UP NOT A CAREER.

THE STREETS WILL ALWAYS HAVE A FRESH ROTATION OF HUSTLERS AND THE GAME DON'T STOP IF YOU'RE NO LONGER IN IT.

"LARRY LOVE EM-ALL" IS A SQUARE THAT EVERY

WOMAN HE MEETS IS THE GIRL OF HIS DREAMS.

IF SHE HAS ONE THING IN COMMOM WITH HIM, THAT'S HIS SOULMATE, 'YOU USE KLEENEX TO WIPE YOUR NOSE, THE ONE WITH ALOE VERA.

SO DO I ...YOU'RE MY SOULMATE !'

TIME AFTER TIME THE GIRL OF HIS DREAMS TURNED INTO HIS NIGHTMARES. CUPID MUST HAVE SHOT EVERY BOW IN YOUR ASS, LOVE HAS PUT A SERIOUS HURTING ON YOUR WALLET AND CREDIT CARDS.

THAT BREEZY STILL DRIVING THAT CAR YOU BOUGHT HER AND SHE DOESN'T SPEAK TO YOU ANYMORE, NOT TO MENTION THAT STRIPPER "DESTINY", WHO SOLD YOU A FANTASY ABOUT YOU BEING THE MAN OF HER DREAMS, BUT YOU CAN ONLY SEE HER AT THE STRIP CLUB...HUNDREDS OF DOLLARS AND DOZENS OF LAP DANCES LATER SHE STILL HAS NEVER EVEN TALKED TO YOU OUTSIDE THE CLUB.

BUT Y'ALL ARE DATING RIGHT ?

SHE'S FEEDING A FOOL FANTASIES, BY ROLE PLAYING LET ME PUT YOU UP ON GAME LARRY, WOMEN SMELL A SUCKER A MILE AWAY, YOU'RE WEARING A COLOGNE CALLED "EASY MARK."

SEE A SUCKER, TAKE A SUCKER, FEED HIM FANTASIES. I SUGGEST YOU TAKE A LOOK AT YOURSELF AND THE LAST FEW RELATIONSHIPS. WHAT DID NOT WORK, WHERE WERE YOU TOO NAÏVE, WHAT WAS THE END RESULT, ALL THE PROOF YOU NEED WILL PRESENT ITSELF, THEN IT'S UP TO YOU TO LEARN FROM YOUR EXPERIENCES AND ADJUST YOUR GAME PLAN, HERE IS A LIFE LESSON FROM

ME, "MONEY DAMN SURE DOESN'T BUY LOVE!"
IT BUYS MOMENTARY SATISFACTION …………..

"MISTER WORK HARD ALL THE TIME!"
ALWAYS LEAVING YOUR WOMAN ALONE THINKING BECAUSE YOU PAY THE BILLS, SHE'S HAPPY. THEN YOU WONDER HOW YOUR BEST FRIEND ENDED UP IN YOUR BED,

IT'S BECAUSE YOU WERE NOT IN IT...

BALANCE IS THE KEY TO LIFE AND LOVE, MAKE TIME FOR HER, INCLUDE HER IN SOME OF THE THINGS YOU DO, LET HER HANDLE SOME OF THE THINGS YOU DO.

SHE NEEDS YOU NOT YOUR WALLET, YOUR WALLET IS ONLY IMPORTANT IF SHE'S A GOLD DIGGER.

GIVE A LITTLE ATTENTION GAIN A LOT OF LOVE .

GANGSTAS, GANGSTERS, HUSTLERS, BANGERS, SOME OF YOU CATS JUST STAY MEAN MUGGING, GANGSTA AT BREAKFAST, GANGSTA AT LUNCH, GANGSTA AT DINNER, JUST ALL ABOUT YOUR HOOD, YOUR HUSTLE, GANGSTA WHEN YOU GETTING LAID, LMAO, LOL, ROTF, HA HA, DAWG YOUR WOMAN IS A FOREGONE CONCLUSION JUST WAITING FOR TO BE CHOSEN BY A PLAYA.

SHE NEEDS A SMILE SOMETIMES, A HUG, JUST SOME AFFECTION, YEAH, SHE MAYBE A GANGSTA CHICK TOO BUT SHE'S STILL A GIRL, AND EVERY WOMAN IS BUILT ON EMOTIONS, MY PLAYA PARTNER 'RITCHIE' WOULD SAY "PUT A BOW ON HER, THAT'S MY GIFT!"

EASE UP ON THE G-CODE AND GIVE HER SOME LOVE SOMETIMES.

"MR DO RIGHT !"

SO SAVED, SO HOLY, SO SANCTIFIED, WHEN YOU MET HER SHE WAS A HARLOT, HER LACE KNEE HIGHS CAUGHT YOUR ATTENTION HER THONGS TURNED YOU ON, YOU LUSTED, YOU PURSUED, YOU LOVED THE WAY SHE COULD POP THAT THANG, SHE NIBBLED ON YOUR EAR, LICKED THE BACK OF YOUR NECK, EVERY HAIR ON YOUR BODY STOOD UP, SHE JUST TURNED YOU OUT.

NOW SUDDENLY YOU WANT HER TO CHANGE. NO MORE MINI SKIRTS, NO SHOWING HER CLEAVAGE, NO MORE PUSH UP BRAS, HER BODY HAS TAKEN CONTROL OF YOUR THOUGHTS.

THE GREEN EYED MONSTER OF JEALOUSY HAS WRAPPED ITSELF AROUND YOU, SHE IS A FREAK ON A LEASH, "SPANK ME DADDY !"

THE WORDS HAVE YOU GONE, NOSE WIDE OPEN, YOU THOUGHT YOU COULD TAME HER, THIS FORCE OF NATURE, WAITING TO BE UNLEASHED, THEN LOOK OUT WORLD.

BORING SISTER JENKINS DOWN THE BLOCK HAS BEEN TRYING TO GET YOUR ATTENTION FOR YEARS, AT CHURCH, AT PRAYER MEETINGS, AT COMMUNITY EVENTS, EVEN THE PASTOR KNOWS SISTER JENKINS HAS A THING FOR YOU.

BUT YOU ACT LIKE YOU DON'T NOTICE, WHY?

I'LL TELL YOU WHY, SHE DOESN'T MAKE YOUR PULSE RACE, HER SKIRTS ARE TOO LONG SHE ACTS TOO CONSERVATIVE, SHE'S TOO SAFE. SO WHY IS IT THAT YOU WANT YOUR HARLOT TO ACT LIKE THAT, DRESS LIKE THAT?

"MR BILLY BIBLE THUMPER."

YOU'RE A CONFLICTED SOUL, YOUR FLESH AND SPIRIT HAVE YOU GOING CRAZY, YOU'VE BEEN PRAYING, SINGING AND SHOUTING BUT NOTHING WORKS, YOUR HEART WANTS WHAT IT WANTS.

HOW DO I KNOW YOU?

THAT HARLOT BEEN DOWN WITH ME FOR YEARS AND WE TALK ABOUT EVERYTHING. WOMEN DO NOT LIKE TO BE JUDGED AND MY FRIEND YOU'RE ON HER LAST NERVE.

SISTER JENKINS IS ALSO GETTING FRUSTRATED BY BEING PUT ON THE SIDELINES BY YOU. I KNOW HER TOO, GOOD GIRLS LIKE BAD BOYS
SHE IS A TALENTED FELLATIO ARTIST, BUT YOU NEVER TOOK THE TIME TO GET TO KNOW HER.

PLAYAS DON'T HATE. WE APPRECIATE ALL THAT A WOMAN HAS TO OFFER.

MISS JENKINS WANTED TO KNOW WHAT THAT HARLOT HAS THAT SHE DOESN'T HAVE. ONE NIGHT AFTER A COUPLE GLASSES OF MERLOT HER WILD SIDE WENT INTO OVERDRIVE.

ME, SISTER JENKINS, AND THE HARLOT HOOKED UP FOR A MENAGE TRIOS. THE QUIET ONES ARE THE FREAKIEST.

SISTER JENKINS PUT IN SOME WORK, (SHOUT OUT TO YOU SJ).

BILLY HERE IS SOME GAME FOR YOU. IF YOU WANT A WOMAN TO BE WITH YOU ACCEPT HER FOR WHO SHE IS, STOP BEATING YOURSELF UP AND MAKING HER FEEL AS THOUGH SHE IS THE REASON FOR YOUR STRUGGLE,

YOU LIKE FREAKY WOMEN, THAT'S IT, THAT'S ALL THERE IS TO IT LET THAT WOMAN GIVE YOU WHAT YOU NEED DAWG.

LET THAT WOMAN BE HERSELF.

NOW LADIES THIS IS FOR YOU

WHAT WOULD LIFE BE WITHOUT YOU?

I'M THE MAN YOUR MOMMA TOLD YOU TO STAY AWAY FROM BUT WAS SEEING ON THE LOW HA HA.

MY CONVERSATION, MY SWAGGER...EVERYTHING SAYS PLAYA. BUT AFTER WE SIT, AND EXCHANGE A FEW WORDS I'M NOT THE BOOGIE MAN YOU WERE TOLD ABOUT.

YOU FEEL COMFORTABLE WITH ME. THIS IS PLEASANTLY SURPRISING TO YOU. YOU CAN SAY ANYTHING YOU WANT TO SAY, BE AS SEXY AND FREAKY AS YOU WANT TO BE.

I MAKE YOUR DRINK THE WAY YOU LIKE.

I KNOW YOUR FAVORITE FRAGRANCE.

I KNOW YOUR FEARS AND FANTASIES.

YOU HATE TO LEAVE AND I HATE TO SEE YOU GO, BUT MY TIME IS TO BE SHARED.

BUT I ALWAYS MAKE TIME FOR YOU.

I TAKE CARE OF YOU.

YOU TAKE CARE OF ME.

FAIR EXCHANGE ISN'T ROBBERY.

PUTTING LABELS ON WHAT WE SHARE IS NEVER NEEDED, IT JUST IS WHAT IT IS.

LADIES, PLEASE STOP TAKING ADVICE FROM WOMEN WHO HAVE NOTHING GOOD TO SAY ABOUT MEN.

IF SHE HAS NO ONE IN HER LIFE, HOW CAN SHE TELL YOU HOW TO RUN THE RELATIONSHIP YOU HAVE!

WOMEN WHO SPEND TOO MUCH TIME MALE BASHING NEED TO QUESTION THE TYPE OF MEN THEY ATTRACT, OR THE TYPE OF MEN THEY ARE ATTACTED TO.

BUT THEY NEVER DO. IF YOU HAVE BEEN DATING THE SAME GUY IN DIFFERENT BODIES AND EXPECTING SOMETHING DIFFERENT NO ONE IS TO BLAME FOR YOU BEING DELUSIONAL.

EXPAND THE SCOPE OF YOUR VISION AND GIVE SOMETHING NEW A TRY.

ALSO STOP TRYING TO SAY IF A BROTHA DON'T DO THIS HE CAN'T BE WITH ME. IF A BROTHA DON'T DO THAT, HE CAN'T BE WITH ME.

YOU'VE HAD BROTHAS WHO DID THE THINGS YOU LIKED AND YOU'RE STILL SINGLE IN THE CLUB LOOKING FOR LOVE, OR GOING TO CHURCH SAYING YOU'RE WAITING ON THE LORD TO SEND YOU SOMEBODY. C'MON NOW BABYGIRL!

THERE ARE THINGS GOING ON WITH YOU THAT YOU NEED TO ADJUST. SOME OF IT MAY BE DUE TO BAD RELATIONSHIPS BUT AT THE END OF THE DAY IT STILL COMES BACK TO YOU.

THEN SOME OF YOU ARE IN RELATIONSHIPS THAT HAVE NO JOY, NO LOVE, NOTHING, BUT YOU TAKE NO ACTION AND COMPLAIN TO EVERYONE YOU KNOW.

WHY ARE YOU PROLONGING THIS MISERY?

BECAUSE SOMETIMES THE MISERY HAS BECOME A PART OF YOU AND IT IS ALL THAT YOU KNOW.

IT TAKES TWO TO TANGO. FREE YOURSELF. LIFE IS TOO DAMN SHORT, AND MEN ARE PLENTIFUL.

EVEN THOUGH YOU OUTNUMBER US (A FACT I PERSONALLY ENJOY) THERE STILL GOOD BROTHAS OUT THERE. JUST SPEND SOMETIME BETTER QUALIFYING YOUR APPLICANTS.

THERE ARE A LOT OF FAKE BROTHAS OUT THERE PRETENDING TO BE "GENUINE".

BUT AS WITH ANYTHING FAKE IT EVENTUALLY CRACK AND FADES BUT THE REAL DEAL STAYS CONSISTENT.

MEMBERS OF "WOMEN INC."

(BY THE WAY WOMEN INC. IS JUST A NAME I GAVE TO MY SUGA, SUGAS, IT HAS NO AFFILIATION TO ANY BUSINESS BY THAT NAME, LOL).

I'M A MAJOR PARTICIPANT IN THE DAY TO DAY RUNNING OF THIS GLOBAL EMPIRE. THE WORLDWIDE ASSETS ARE IMMEASURABLE. THERE IS NO GREATER COMMODITY ON EARTH. THERE IS NOTHING MORE APPEALING THAN A WELL PUT TOGETHER WOMAN.

WHEN YOU SEE HER, WHEN YOU SPEAK TO HER EVERYTHING, ABOUT HER JUST MOVES YOU.

IN YOUR MIND YOU THINK "GOD BLESS HER PARENTS!" FOR CREATING SOMETHING AS BEAUTIFUL AS YOU. I'M A LIFELONG FAN OF WOMEN. THERE IS NEVER SUCH A THING AS TOO MANY WOMEN.

LADIES, REMEMBER YOU CAN RADIATE BEAUTY FROM WITHIN AND IF A MAN IS FOR YOU THIS WILL BE WHAT HE GRAVITATES TOWARDS.

LUST EVENTUALLY FADES. WHEN A MAN IS FOR YOU, HE'S STILL YOUR BIGGEST FAN ON YOUR WORST DAY. REAL TALK...HE KNOWS HIS LIFE IS BETTER WITH YOU IN IT AND HE SHOWS IT. BE GOOD TO YOUR MAN AND MAKE SURE HE'S GOOD TO YOU.

IF YOU NEED APPRECIATION, MAKE SURE YOU SHOW YOUR MAN YOU APPRECIATE HIM.

I'M GOING TO PUT YOU UP SOME GAME, IF YOU HAVE SOME SOMETHING GOOD LIMIT HOW MUCH YOU TELL YOUR GIRLS ABOUT HIM.

KEEP THEM ON A NEED TO KNOW BASIS. THIS WAS TOLD TO ME BY WOMEN THAT WERE BETRAYED BY FRIENDS.

WHY WOULD YOU LET ANYONE DEEP INTO YOUR PERSONAL AFFAIRS ANYWAYS? I'M ROLLING WITH THE LADIES RIGHT NOW. NEVER RUSH TO START A RELATIONSHIP. LET IT BREATHE AND GROW.

AND PLEASE STOP MOVING MEN INTO YOUR HOME TOO QUICKLY, ESPECIALLY IF YOU HAVE CHILDREN.

DON'T LET YOUR NEED FOR AN ORGASM OR COMPANY CLOUD YOUR JUDGEMENT.

SOMETIMES WHEN YOU RUSH INTO THINGS YOUR

CHILDREN BEAR THE SCARS OR THE MAN FEELS LIKE YOU TRYING TO SIGN HIM UP FOR "DADDY DUTY!"

SLOW YOUR ROLL BABYGIRL.

KNOW WHAT POSITION THE MAN WANTS IN YOUR LIFE AND MAKE SURE YOU KNOW WHAT POSITION YOU'RE LOOKING FOR AND IF HE'S WILLING TO GIVE IT TO YOU.

DON'T GO TO FANTASY LAND AND START IMAGINING THINGS THAT ARE NOT THERE.

OKAY LADIES I MUST TAKE LEAVE OF YOUR COMPANY, BUT PLEASE KNOW THAT THERE IS NOT A MOMENT OF THE DAY I DON'T THINK ABOUT YOU .

NOW FELLAS I'M BACK WITH YOU AGAIN .

HMMMMMMMMM…
WHERE WAS I ? WHATEVER!

PLAYAOSOPHY....

ALWAYS MAKE A WOMAN FEEL
RELEVANT TO YOUR LIFE.

NEVER TAKE HER KINDNESS FOR GRANTED.
(EG: DO NOT HAVE ANOTHER WOMAN
DRIVING THE CAR SHE BOUGHT YOU).

TAKE NOTICE OF HER NEW HAIRSTYLES.

LET HER KNOW THAT HER NEW OUTFIT
LOOKS GOOD ON HER
"YOU GO GIRL!"
TAKE A FEW MOMENTS TO SIT AND
TALK TO HER AND LISTEN TO HER.

BE ATTENTIVE TO HER WHEN
HER FRIENDS ARE AROUND.
(WOMEN SECRETLY LIKE TO GLOAT ON THE INSIDE).

WHEN YOU'RE IN PUBLIC KEEP YOUR EYES ON HER.
(STRAYING EYES ARE VERY INSULTING TO A WOMAN).

ALRIGHT LET'S MOVE ON TO "MR SENSITIVITY"...

YOU MY FRIEND ARE A SPECIAL BREED, AND YOU CATS JUST TICKLE ME. IF YOU LIKE A WOMAN, TELL HER!

YOU CARRY THESE FEELINGS. YOUR FEELINGS LOCKED UP IN YOUR HEART FOR WEEKS, MONTHS,YEARS...JUST WAITING IN THE WINGS, WATCHING, WAITING, AND SADLY AS THE TIME GOES BY YOUR WINDOW OF OPPURTUNITY GETS SMALLER AND SMALLER.

YOU HAVE BEEN PRETENDING TO BE HER FRIEND FOR

YEARS AND SHE STILL DOES NOT KNOW THE WAY YOU FEEL.

YOU'VE GOTTEN TO KNOW HER AND YOU STILL HAVE NOT STEPPED UP. ARE YOU WAITING TO BE STRUCK BY LIGHTNING?

SOMETIMES SOME OF YOU CATS CARRY THESE FEELINGS FOR YEARS, LOSE TRACK OF THE GIRL AND STILL NEVER ONCE TOOK A CHANCE TO STEP OUT ON FAITH.

SOME OTHER MAN IS GOING TO GET HER, AND YET YOU REMAIN HIDDEN. IF YOU DON'T EXPRESS YOURSELF, YOU WILL SPEND MANY LONELY NIGHTS BUILDING UP YOUR ARM STRENGTH, AND THE PALM OF YOUR HAND WILL BE SOFTER BECAUSE OF A WHOLE LOT OF MOISTURE...LOL!

ALL YOU KEEP WORRYING ABOUT IS THE REJECTION. 'SUPPOSE SHE DOESN'T LIKE ME?'

THAT IS A POSSIBILITY.

BUT HOW MUCH MORE DIFFERENT WOULD THAT BE THAN YOU SITTING AROUND WONDERING, WANTING HER, FANTASIES CAN BECOME VERY POWERFUL, 'A CLOSED MOUTH DON'T GET FED!'

OKAY MR SENSITIVITY, HERE IS SOME GAME FOR YOUR ASS. BEFORE YOU MAKE YOUR MOVE GET YOUR GAME FACE ON. PRACTICE WHAT YOU'RE GOING TO SAY, SO THAT YOU DON'T APPEAR TO BE A BABBLING FOOL.

MAKE HER AWARE OF THE FACT YOU LIKE HER BUT DO NOT COME OFF LIKE YOU'RE OBSESSED. "DO NOT GO OVERBOARD". YOU'RE PLANTING SEEDS IN HER MIND THAT NEED TIME TO GROW. SHE HAS OTHER THINGS GOING ON SO JUST BE COOL. IF YOU REALLY LIKE THIS

WOMAN YOU'VE GOTTEN TO KNOW SOME THINGS ABOUT HER. INCORPORATE THEM INTO YOUR GAMEPLAN.

BE EASY, EVEN THOUGH THAT'S HARD BECAUSE YOU DREAM ABOUT HER SHARPEN YOUR IMAGE, MAKE YOURSELF MORE APPEALING.

NOW PLEASE UNDERSTAND THAT SHE STILL MAY NOT WANT YOU BUT THE GOOD NEWS IS THAT BY STEPPING UP YOU GREW AS A MAN AND NEXT TIME YOU WILL BE MORE CONFIDENT AND SOMEONE ELSE WILL NOTICE THE CHANGE IN YOU.

SWAGGER IS EXTREMELY IMPORTANT.
YOU HAVE SPENT YOUR WHOLE LIFE PLAYING THE SIDELINES, IT'S TIME TO GET IN THE GAME.

PLAYAOSOPHY

VERBAL SKILLS ARE A PRIMARY REQUIREMENT OF THIS LIFESTYLE.

KEEPING A CONVERSATION ON POINT AND EXPRESSING YOUR INTENTIONS ARE NEEDED SO THAT ALL PARTIES INVOLVED ARE ON THE SAME PAGE.

YOUR COMPANY IS SOMETHING A WOMAN SHOULD WANT. SOMETHING SHE THINKS ABOUT, SOMETHING SHE DESIRES.

LEAVE A FAVORABLE IMPRESSION ON HER AND SHE WILL YEARN FOR YOUR COMPANY.

LEARN HOW TO 'SPEAK EASY'. A LAID BACK TONE OF VOICE, AN EASY GOING STYLE, A REASSURING WAY ABOUT YOURSELF.

THIS BOND SHE FEELS WITH YOU IS DEEPER THAN SEX. IT IS MENTAL, SPIRITUAL.

TO TRULY LIVE THIS LIFE YOU MUST REPROGRAM YOUR MIND AND ONCE YOU START OPERATING BY THE PLAYAS CODE IT BECOMES ENGRAINED IN YOU.

ONE DAY YOU WILL MEET A GIRL THAT FLIPS YOU UPSIDE DOWN AND YOUR HEART AND SOUL WILL BOND WITH HER, BUT YOUR PLAYAS MINDSET WILL NOT LET YOU COMMIT TO HER THE WAY YOU SHOULD.

THIS IS THE MAJOR SIDE EFFECT OF BEING ONE OF US. YOU WILL STRUGGLE WITH THIS AND IT MIGHT COST YOU THE LOVE OF YOUR LIFE. THIS IS PART OF THE GAME NOBODY TELLS YOU ABOUT

BUT I'M A GENUINE PLAYA. SO I PRESENT THINGS AS THEY ARE.

SOMETIMES YOU'RE LUCKY ENOUGH TO FIND A GIRL THAT ACCEPTS YOU UNCONDITIONALLY, DESPITE THE FACTS AND CIRCUMSTANCES OF YOUR LIFE. SHE ENDURES YOUR FLIRTATIOUS WAYS, DIMISSES SOME OF YOUR DISCRETIONS, SHE HOLDS DOWN THE HOME FRONT AND DOES NOT HESITATE TO PROTECT HER TERRITORY. SHE IS YOUR RIB.

HER 'MAN' IS HER FOCUS. SHE IS FIERCELY LOYAL. IF YOU'RE LUCKY ENOUGH TO FIND HER CEMENT HER PLACE IN YOUR LIFE. DO NOT TAKE HER FOR GRANTED. MAKE SURE EVERYBODY PLAYS THEIR POSITION THIS KIND OF WOMAN IS TRULY ONE IN A MILLION. 'I TIP MY HAT TO YOU, BABY!'

BEING A PLAYA IS NOT FOR EVERYBODY. SO MANY CLAIM THE TITLE, YET THEY DON'T KNOW THE HISTORY OF BEING A PLAYA. AND NO I'M NOT TALKING ABOUT PIMPING OR MOVIES LIKE THE 'MACK'.

I'M TALKING ABOUT DON JUAN/DON GIOVANNI (NOT THE BISHOP...CHUUUCH) CASANOVA, KING MONGUT OF SIAM, SOLOMON, KING DAVID, AKUKU DANGER, A LONG HISTORY OF LOTHARIOS, THRU THE AGES.

GENTLEMEN PLAYAS PLAY, THAT IS WHAT WE DO. WE DON'T PLAY GAMES, BUT WE PLAY THE GAME. LET THAT MARINATE WITH YOU FOR A MOMENT.

WHAT IS YOUR MOTIVATION ?
DO YOU JUST WANT TO BE A PLAYA BECAUSE IT SEEMS COOL? OR IS THAT SOMEONE BROKE YOUR HEART AND NOW YOU HAVE INSECURITIES?

BETTER THEM THAN ME IS NOW YOUR MANTRA BUT DID YOU EVER STOP TO THINK THAT THIS LIFESTYLE IS A DOUBLE EDGED SWORD? AND YOU HAVE TO TAKE THE GOOD AND THE BAD OF IT .

THE FACT OF THE MATTER IS THAT BY DATING MULTIPLE WOMEN CERTAIN RISK FACTORS ARE MULTIPLED.

PREGNANCIES, EXPOSURE TO SEXUALLY TRANSMITTED DISEASES, STALKERS, ABORTIONS, DRAMA, JEALOUS BOYFRIENDS, JEALOUS GIRLFRIENDS, ETC., ETC.

OH LET US NOT FORGET CHILD SUPPORT.

I TOLD YOU CATS THAT I KEEP IT REAL...

WE SAY AND DO THINGS THAT OTHER MEN ONLY DREAM ABOUT. SO THAT BRINGS OUT THE 'HATERS'.

THEY SAY A PLAYA IS NOT ON TOP OF HIS GAME IF HE DOESN'T HAVE HATERS. THEY SO BUSY SPITTING VENOM THAT THEY POISON THEIR OWN GAME AND THE LOSS OF FOCUS MAKES THEIR VISION BLURRY.

BUT A PLAYAS JOB IS TO SHINE, SO BLIND THEIR ASS BUT KEEP AN EYE ON THEM BECAUSE THEY SOMETIIMES TRY TO GET FROGGY.

NOW SOMETIMES WE HAVE CERTAIN FRIENDS OR ASSOCIATES THAT WE KEEP AROUND AND THEY ARE BLOCKING US FROM OUR SUCCESS TAKE A GOOD LOOK AROUND YOU.

SHAKE OFF THE ZEREOS.

ASSOCIATE WITH PEOPLE MAKIN MOVES TO CLIMB THE SOCIAL LADDER. GET MOTIVATED. 'PLAYAS PARTICIPATE

NOT PROCRASTINATE' AND TO PARTICIPATE TAKE A DOSE OF 'ACT RIGHT'. KEEP BULLSHIT TO A MINIMAL AND CHOOSE VERY CAREFULLY WHO YOU LET INTO YOUR INNER CIRCLE.

DO THOSE AROUND YOU SPEAK THE UNIVERSAL PLAYA LANGUAGE, 'DOLLANESE'?

THE FINER THINGS IN LIFE REQUIRE FINANCIAL GROWTH, FRUITFUL ENDEAVORS, FISCAL DISCIPLINE.

SO WAKE UP, SHAKE UP, GET WHERE YOU NEED TO BE, AND USE YOU BRAIN TO WORK SMARTER NOT HARDER.

THERE ARE NO FREE RIDERS ON THE MONEY TRAIN.

NOW BACK TO THE LESSON AT HAND,

SOME BROTHERS OUT THERE ARE NOT QUITE SURE WHAT IT IS YOU REQUIRE FROM YOUR SIGNIFICANT OTHER AND YOU DECIDE TO CREEP AROUND.

YOU HAVE A GOOD WOMAN BUT YOU FAIL TO SEE THE TREASURE BEFORE YOU, AND SO YOU WANT TO TIPPY TOE INTO MY WORLD AND BE AN 'UNDERCOVER PLAYA' AND AS WITH ANYTHING IN LIFE WHEN YOU LACK THE SKILLS REQUIRED OR THE RULES OF THE GAME YOU FAIL AND GET CAUGHT.

NOW YOU'VE BECOME 'MR. PLEASE BABY PLEASE' AND SHE'S SHOWING YOU THAT TWO CAN PLAY THAT GAME.

WAS IT REALLY WORTH IT?

IN CASE I DIDN'T MENTION IT BEFORE WOMEN ARE THE BEST AT BEING PLAYAS, THAT IS WHERE I TRULY

LEARNED TO BE A PLAYA.

SO THE QUESTION IS NOW WHAT ARE THE CREEPING COMMANDMENTS?

CREEPING COMMANDMENTS

NEVER CREEP AROUND WITH ANYONE OF A LESSER CALIBER THAN WHAT YOU HAVE AT HOME.
IF THAT SIDE BREEZY IS NOT DAYLIGHT MATERIAL HIT IT ONCE AND QUIT IT.
NEVER, EVER, EVER, BRING YOUR SIDE BREEZY TO YOUR HOME, WHERE YOU AND WIFEY RESIDE, THIS IS AN ABSOLUTE NO NO, NOT EVER, EVER.
ALWAYS HAVE A COUPLE OUTFITS AT YOUR HOMBOYS' HOUSE, SO YOU CAN CHANGE FOR YOUR RENDEVOUS, ALWAYS COME HOME IN WHAT YOU LEFT THE HOUSE WEARING.
NEVER GO TO THE HANGOUTS AND PLACES THAT YOU AND WIFEY FREQUENT.
KEEP A SEPARATE PREPAID CELL PHONE, THAT NEVER COMES NEAR YOUR HOME.
IF YOUR SIDE BREEZY HAS YOUR PERSONAL NUMBER MAKE SURE YOU KEEP HER ON A SHORT LEASH, BLOWIN YOUR PHONE UP IS NEVER ACCEPTABLE.
WOMEN ARE NATURAL DETECTIVES, THEY KNOW YOUR PATTERNS, AND ANY CHANGES ARE QUICKLY IDENTIFIED.
DO NOT START TAKING SHOWERS WHEN YOU COME HOME IF YOU NEVER DID THAT BEFORE.
DO NOT START PUSHING HER AWAY WHEN YOU HAVE ALWAYS CUDDLED WITH HER.
DO NOT SUDDENLY BECOME RELUCTANT TO DO THE THINGS SHE LIKES.
NEVER WEAR YOURSELF OUT ON YOUR SIDE

BREEZY, SO YOU CANT PERFORM AT HOME.
STAY AWAY FROM THE TEMPTATION TO CREEP IN YOUR IMMEDIATE ENVIRONMENT, IT IS TOO CLOSE TO HOME, STAY AWAY FROM THE FREAKY FRIEND, THE FLIRTY COUSIN, THE SEXY NEIGHBOUR, THAT ARE ALWAYS DROPPING HINTS.
WOMEN LOVE TO PUT MEN IN TRAPS.
FAMILIARITY BREEDS CONTEMPT, THESE WOMEN ARE ALWAYS AROUND AND CAN CAUSE PROBLEMS.
THEY START GETTING FEELINGS, SO THEY START GETTING SNEAKY.
THEY HAVE ACCESS TO YOUR WIFEY AND YOUR HOME, THEY CAN LEAVE STRANDS OF HAIR IN YOUR BATHROOM, WEARING EXTRA PERFUME TO MAKE SURE THEY LEAVE A SCENT IN YOUR CAR OR COUCH.
FORGETTING UNDERWEAR IN YOUR HOME OR CAR.
PUTTING THEIR NAIL POLISH IN WITH YOUR WIFEYS'.
DROPPING LIPSTICK IN A ODD CORNER.
MAKING DEMANDS FOR MORE TIME AND TRYING TO BLACKMAIL YOU, COMPARING WHAT YOU DO FOR WIFEY TO WHAT YOU DO FOR HER.
NEVER LOSE THE FOCUS ON YOUR HOME.
PAY CASH FOR ALL OF YOUR CREEPING ACTIVITIES, NEVER TAKE RECIEPTS.
ALWAYS CHECK YOUR POCKETS, LEAVE NO PAPERTRAIL.
NO CONDOMS IN YOUR POCKET, ESPECIALLY IF YOU DO NOT USE THEM AT HOME. IF YOU USE THEM AT HOME ALWAYS PURCHASE THAT BRAND, REMEMBER WIFEY COUNTS THE CONDOMS, BUT IF YOU SLIP UP HAVING THE SAME BRAND IS EASIER TO EXPLAIN.
KEEP WIFEY ACTIVE AND HAPPY.

KEEP UNFLATTERING COMMENTS TO YOUR DAMN SELF.
IF YOU HAVE A YOUNGER SIDE BREEZY, DO NOT START COMPARING THE TWO WOMEN, BECAUSE YOU WILL THEN SAY SOMETHING OUT OF LINE AND THIS WILL TRIGGER THE NATURAL DETECTIVE IN WIFEY.
HAVE AN EXTRA EMAIL ACCOUNT THAT YOU NEVER CHECK AT HOME.
WOMEN ARE BETTER AT CREEPING SO THEY KNOW WHAT TO LOOK FOR.
WHEN YOU CLEAR TEXT MESSAGES, MAKE SURE YOU CLEAR INBOX AND OUTBOX.
IF YOU'RE STARTING TO CATCH FEELINGS FOR THE SIDE BREEZY, IT'S TIME TO WALK AWAY, THIS RULE ONLY APPLIES IF WIFEY IS PLAYING HER POSITION, IF SHE SLIPPIN TELL HER KICK ROCKS.
NEVER BUY THE SAME GIFTS FOR THE WOMEN IN YOUR LIFE.
NEVER TAKE YOUR KIDS AROUND THE SIDE BREEZY.
NEVER MAKE OR TAKE CALLS ON YOUR HOME PHONE.
BEFORE YOU BECOME AN UNDERCOVER PLAYA, THINK ABOUT IT CAREFULLY.
WHILE YOU'RE TRYING TO DO YOUR THING ANOTHER MAN ALWAYS WANTS WHAT YOU HAVE, TRUST ME.
KNOW THAT THE WOMAN YOU LIVE WITH KNOWS THE INTIMATE DETAILS OF YOUR LIFE AND CAN WREAK HAVOC ON YOUR LIFE.
NEVER EVER THINK YOU'RE SMARTER THAN HER. ALWAYS ASSUME SHE HAS GAME TOO AND THIS WILL KEEP YOU ON YOUR TOES.
SUNRISE SHOULD NEVER CATCH YOU WITH YOUR CREEPIN PARTNER, GO HOME, YOUR CREEPIN PARTNER SHOULD KNOW THEIR POSITION AND

PLAY THAT ROLE.
AN OLD SCHOOL PLAYA ONCE TOLD ME "YOUNGBLOOD" IF YOU GOT A GOOD WOMAN AT HOME NEVER GET INVOLVED WITH ANOTHER WOMAN YOU CAN'T WALK AWAY FROM TOMORROW.
WHEN YOU START TO CREEP YOU MUST LAY OUT THE RULES TO THE SIDE BREEZY, IF SHE SETS THE RULES YOU WILL BE IN FOR A ROLLER COASTER RIDE.
KEEP YOUR EGO IN CHECK, THE MORE THINGS RUN SMOOTHLY, YOU WILL START FEELING LIKE 'YEAH I'M THE MAN.' THIS IS WHEN YOU WILL START TO MAKE MISTAKES.
WHAT IS YOUR EXIT STRATEGY IF SHIT HITS THE FAN, WIFEY IS GOING TO COME OUT SWINGING HARD...DO YOU HAVE ANY CASH STASHED AWAY, A PREPAID CREDIT CARD THAT DOES NOT SHOW UP ON YOUR CREDIT REPORT THAT YOU LOAD MONEY ON?
HAVE YOU BEEN PRACTICING WHAT TO SAY IN VARIOUS HEATED ARGUMENTS.
KEEP A BOTTLE OF 'FEBREEZE' IN YOUR TRUNK AT ALL TIMES IT IS GREAT AT REMOVING SCENTS OUT OF YOUR CAR SEAT AND ALSO ALWAYS CLEAN THE SEATBELTS.
NEVER EVER LEAVE SIDE BREEZY ALONE IN YOUR CAR, YOUR CAR REGISTRATION AND INSURANCE CONTAINS PERSONAL INFO, AND YOUR GLOVEBOX ALWAYS HAS STUFF THAT SHOWS YOUR LIFE.
PUT YOUR WALLET AND CAR INFORMATION IN YOUR TRUNK OR TAKE YOUR PANTS TO THE BATHROOM WHEN YOU'RE SHOWERING.

LEARN THESE COMMANDMENTS. THEY WILL KEEP YOU SAFE BUT NOTHING IS GURANTEED. THE INTERNET HAS CHANGED THE GAME. PLENTY OF WEBSITES WILL SELL YOUR LIFE STORY FOR A PRICE.

THE GAME IS ON A WHOLE DIFFERENT LEVEL SO CHOOSE YOUR CREEPIN PARTNER CAREFULLY AND MAKE SURE SHE WANTS TO PLAY THE GAME YOU'RE OFFERING.

NOW MOVING ON.

A MAN MUST BE THE KING OF HIS DOMAIN BUT HIS QUEENS' INPUT SHOULD BE VITAL TO HIM. ALWAYS REMEMBER WOMEN ARE VERY GOOD AT "PASSIVE RESISTANCE" SO BE CAREFUL HOW MUCH YOU RAIN ON HER PARADE.

SHE CAN CARRY A GRUDGE FOR A LONG TIME AND WAIT FOR HER MOMENT TO ROCK YOUR WORLD. KEEP YOUR DOMAIN AS HARMONIOUS AS POSSIBLE. RESTRICT TOO MANY PEOPLE JUST RUNNING ALL UP IN YOUR PERSONAL SPACE, BUT BE SURE YOUR WIFEY IS ABLE TO SPREAD HER WINGS AND FLY.

WHAT DO YOU LOVE ABOUT ME ?

I LOVE YOUR MIND FOR EVERY BEAUTIFUL
THOUGHT IT CREATES,

I LOVE YOUR EYES
FOR THE LOVING WAY IT LOOKS AT ME,

I LOVE YOUR HANDS
FOR THE GENTLE WAY THEY TOUCH ME,

I LOVE YOUR LIPS
FOR THE LOVE THEY EXPRESS TO ME
AND THE KISSES THEY GIVE TO ME

I LOVE YOUR LEGS
FOR EVERY STEP THEY TAKE TO
BRING YOU TO ME,

MOST OF ALL I LOVE YOUR
SOUL FOR BONDING WITH MINE
AND MAKING ME WHOLE .

DING DING. MY LECTURE HAS CONCLUDED AND I'VE LAID THE GAME OUT THERE FOR YOU AS RAW AS I COULD AND I HOPE THAT MY TRUTH WILL RESONATE WITH SOME BODY OUT THERE.

DON'T TRIP VOLUME III IS GONNA BE THE MASTERS DEGREE. REMEMBER THAT BEING A 'PLAYA' IS ABOUT LEARNING TO PLAY THE GAME OF LIFE AND THE GAME OF LIFE IS WAY BIGGER THAN CHASIN SKIRTS.